WHY EUROPE FAILED

OLIVER HARTWICH

**THE
NEW ZEALAND
INITIATIVE**

connorcourt

Connor Court Publishing Pty Ltd

PO Box 224W
Ballarat VIC 3350
sales@connorcourt.com
www.connorcourt.com

ISBN: 978-1-925138-75-7 (pbk.)

Printed in Australia

The New Zealand Initiative

THE
NEW ZEALAND
INITIATIVE

The New Zealand Initiative is an independent public policy think tank supported by chief executives of major New Zealand businesses. We believe in evidence-based policy and are committed to developing policies that work for all New Zealanders.

Our mission is to help build a better, stronger New Zealand. We are taking the initiative to promote a prosperous, free and fair society with a competitive, open and dynamic economy. We develop and contribute bold ideas that will have a profound, positive, long-term impact.

ABOUT THE AUTHOR

Oliver Hartwich is the Executive Director of The New Zealand Initiative. Before joining the Initiative he was a Research Fellow at the Centre for Independent Studies in Sydney, the Chief Economist at Policy Exchange in London, and an advisor in the UK House of Lords. Oliver holds a Master's degree in Economics and Business Administration and a Ph.D. in Law from Bochum University in Germany.

He has been covering the European crisis as a weekly columnist for the Australian magazine *Business Spectator* since February 2010.

ACKNOWLEDGEMENTS

The author wishes to thank Dr Eric Crampton and Roger Partridge for their comments on this essay, Mollica Sokhom for her design work and Mangai Pitchai for her wonderful editorial assistance. The usual caveats apply.

Oliver Hartwich has written a compelling essay, *Why Europe Failed*. He lucidly identifies the essentially undemocratic character of much of the European project. Political elites, unaccountable to national electorates, impose decisions on tens of millions of people without any real fear of rebuke. Hartwich provides a sobering analysis of an ageing Europe, overburdened by the size of its welfare state. This gives added context to the current travails of Greece.

Sydney, July 2015

Hon John Howard OM AC
Former Prime Minister of Australia

CONTENTS

INTRODUCTION

There was a time, not long ago, when some commentators believed Europe was a model for the rest of the world. US sociologist Jeremy Rifkin forecast *The European Dream: How Europe's Vision of the Future is Quietly Eclipsing the American Dream* (2004); British foreign policy expert Mark Leonard explained *Why Europe Will Run the 21st Century* (2005); and US publicist T.R. Read boldly predicted *The United States of Europe: The New Superpower and the End of American Supremacy* (2004).

A decade later, it would be unthinkable for anyone to write such books. The global financial crisis of 2007/08 may have started in the US with the collapse of its subprime housing market. However, the crisis quickly spread to Europe, where it had far worse consequences. Whereas in the US, the economic crisis mainly affected individual companies such as the failed investment bank Lehman Brothers and insurance giant AIG, the economic crisis in Europe quickly became a crisis of sovereigns. Greece has been teetering on the brink of bankruptcy since late 2009. Ireland, Spain, Portugal and Cyprus had to be bailed out by various mechanisms. France and Italy hardly look reassuring, either.

Some might argue that Europe's recent troubles are just of a cyclical nature and that eventually the continent will recover. However, such an optimistic assessment is not warranted. What we are witnessing in Europe is much more fundamental.

The current troubles of Europe are symptoms of the end of the European world order. To put this into perspective, we only need to think back to the Great War whose centenary we are commemorating.

World War I was the time when Europe last ruled the world politically and economically. The end of that war marked the beginning of the end of Europe's global hegemony – along with a significant era of history.

No doubt history was made in Europe before the Great War. With the Age of Enlightenment, Europe led the way in scientific discoveries and ideas. Industrialisation catapulted Europe's economies from medieval production methods to modernity within a few decades. The military power of European nations was unmatched. Many European nations, even small ones such as Belgium, established colonies all over the world.

On the eve of World War I, Western Europe accounted for one-seventh of the global population but one-third of the global economy. Of the ten largest economies in the world in 1913, six were European.[1] Europe's influence on global ideas and institutions was greater still, not least due to its colonial outreach.

A century ago, European capitals dominated world politics. The streets of London, Paris and Berlin were once the corridors of world power. Indeed, the monumental buildings along Whitehall, the Élysée Palace and the Reichstag still exude a profound sense of greatness and historic significance.

In some ways, this European dominance of world affairs remains palpable to this day. Among the most influential newspapers and broadcasters are the *Financial Times*, *The Economist* and the BBC, all headquartered in London. Europe accounts for three of the UN Security Council's five permanent, veto-power holding members – Britain, France and Russia (not India, Brazil or Japan). Eurocentrism is even more pronounced in the G7, which includes Britain, Germany, France, Italy and the European Union (but not Mexico, Australia or China).

Europe's decay is mostly due to the way Europe has been conducting itself.

But these are the dying embers of a past world behemoth. Europe's influence is undoubtedly in decline. Whereas in 1980, the current 28 EU member states accounted for almost a third of the global economy, their share today is only 23%.[2] Because of the continuing rise of Asian economies, this figure will further decline over the coming decades.

It would be easy to excuse Europe's relative decline as a result of the rise of other, previously poor countries. But that would be dishonest. Europe's decay is mostly due to the way Europe has been conducting itself.

If other countries were catching up with Europe while Europe itself was doing fine, that would be no reason for concern. Such convergence is the rightful triumph of a globalised economy.

But Europe is not doing fine.

Europe's downfall will also show in population numbers. The UN estimates that by 2100, only 5.9% of the world's population will be European compared to the approximately 10% now. This is not just a relative reduction but also an absolute decline of 104 million Europeans from 743 million today to just 639 million in 2100.[3]

Contrast this with the only one statistic in which Europe leads the world by a mile: The EU's 28 member states account for 54% of global spending on social welfare.[4]

It would be optimistic to say Europe is at the crossroads today.

It would be too simplistic to reduce Europe's challenges to problems with its monetary union. Nor is Europe's crisis limited to countries like Greece that produce negative headlines at regular intervals.

Europe's problems are more fundamental. Its elitist structure of governance has locked its political institutions into paralysis. Its economic model of a mixed market economy is unable to keep up pace with more dynamic world regions. Its demographic changes will test the limits of its expanding welfare state. And all of this is happening against a background of increased security concerns on Europe's borders with Africa, the Arab world, and Russia. Europe is being challenged on many fronts at once, and even this is an understatement.

It would be optimistic to say Europe is at the crossroads today. At least that would suggest it has a choice between reform and decline. But it increasingly looks as if there is no such choice and Europe's inevitable future is one of decaying power, wealth and influence.

Europe then is not at the crossroads but is facing a dead-end. Or a cliff. A very steep cliff.

Europe's leaders are struggling to come up with solutions to these challenges, preferring instead to instinctively cling to the EU's mantra of "ever closer union" – as if that programmatic vision, spelt out in the EU Treaty, is sufficient in itself. Or as if "ever closer union" had been a pure success story.

This essay provides a brief historic account of Europe's downfall and an analysis of Europe's current economic and monetary crisis.

More importantly, it tries to make sense of Europe's downfall. If you will, it is a eulogy written for a continent that shaped world history for centuries but is desperately failing to shape its own future. This essay does so from the perspective of a writer who is European himself but has chosen to observe European affairs from the distance of the South Pacific. As such, the account is coloured as much by personal affections and affiliations as by an emotional detachment that such geographical distance allows.

Finally, though there are elements of Europe's decline that are unique to the continent, there are lessons that apply beyond Europe. We in Australasia could do well to learn from the pitfalls of elitist decision-making and an unsustainable, expanding welfare state.

To be clear, Europe is still one of the most developed, most prosperous, and most liveable places on earth. However, the cracks in Europe are clearly visible and will become increasingly pronounced over the coming decades. It is a world region that made the past but will not make the future.

SOME REVISIONIST THOUGHTS ON EUROPEAN INTEGRATION

The official history of European integration is easily told. The attempt to unite Europe came out of the experience of previous conflicts.

The Franco-Prussian War of 1870–71, in which Prussia defeated France, not only paved the way for Germany's first unification. It had also humiliated the French, who had to pay substantial war reparations to Germany and cede the Alsace-Lorraine territory. The result was deep enmity between the two countries.

After World War I, which Germany lost, France not only regained its lost regions but also imposed severe financial conditions on Germany in the Treaty of Versailles. These conditions crippled the German economy and ultimately led to the rise of radical political forces, culminating in World War II.

In both cases, the resolution of wars sowed the seeds of future conflict. The French longed to avenge perceived German injustices after 1871, and it was the other way around in 1918.

Fortunately, there were politicians after World War II who sincerely believed that this vicious cycle had to be broken. They realised that no country should be humiliated and punished following a war defeat because such measures only made the next war more likely. Instead, European countries had to work together to ensure that the horrors of the two world wars were never repeated.

The best expression of this idea is the Schuman Declaration of 1950. Issued by the French government and its foreign minister Robert Schuman, it stated:

> *World peace cannot be safeguarded without the making of creative efforts proportionate to the dangers which threaten it.*
>
> *The contribution which an organized and living Europe can bring to civilization is indispensable to the maintenance of peaceful relations. In taking upon herself for more than 20 years the role of champion of a united Europe, France has always had as her essential aim the service of peace. A united Europe was not achieved and we had war.[5]*

The contrast between past military conflicts on the one hand and European integration on the other is the founding myth of the EU. It is also the motif that European politicians cite whenever problems arise in the governance of European institutions. The message behind it is clear: Yes, integrating European countries is not without its problems. But the alternative is war.

Over the course of European integration, leading politicians like German Chancellor Angela Merkel have often appealed to such reasoning: "No one should think that a further half century of peace and prosperity is assured. If the euro fails, Europe will fail."[6]

As useful as this argument may be for political rhetoric, it is wrong on two grounds. First, it is a *non sequitur* fallacy to proclaim that failure to integrate Europe and to drive this process to an eventual political and economic union would inevitably result in military conflict. There are many neighbouring countries in the world that are not integrated but do not go to war with each other. European integration on its own is not responsible for peace. Without the EU, would Germany invade Austria? Would the Netherlands attack Belgium? Would Sweden conquer Finland? If such questions appear absurd, it is because they are. To claim that without the EU (or even just by weakening the EU) there would be more conflict is rhetorical hyperbole and nothing else.

The second reason to question the EU's founding myth is historical. The EU regards Konrad Adenauer, Joseph Bech, Johan Willem Beyen, Winston Churchill, Alcide De Gasperi, Walter Hallstein, Sicco Mansholt, Jean Monnet, Robert Schuman, Paul-Henri Spaak and Altiero Spinelli as the 'Founding Fathers of the European Union'. The EU says on its website that these men "were a diverse group of people who held the same ideals: a peaceful, united and prosperous Europe."[7]

People like Hallstein and Churchill may have been idealists to some degree. But they were also realists, pragmatists and rationalists –

but most importantly, they were politicians. However genuine, would their commitment to (post-War) peace alone have impelled them to build the EU?

To ask this question is to answer it. It is quite implausible that peace-loving idealism alone would have led to a pan-European integration, otherwise Eastern Europe would have initially been part of the EU and its predecessors. Indeed, the reason Eastern Europe played no role in (Western) European integration is also the real reason for the beginning of European integration after World War II.

The Soviet Union was allied with Western powers in defeating Nazi Germany, but parted ways soon after over the spoils of war. Europe was divided into two spheres of political and ideological influence after 1945. Democracy and capitalism were the guiding ideas in the Western sphere under the United States and Britain, while socialism and central planning ruled in the Eastern sphere under the Soviet Union.

The collision of these two economic and ideological spheres defined European politics from 1945 to 1989. It divided Germany and tore Europe apart.

The European Economic Community (EEC) and its predecessor, the European Coal and Steel Community, were founded in 1957 and 1951, respectively. They were established against this background of increased confrontation between the East and West due to the Cold War and deepening schisms in their spheres of influence. Both the West and East defined their interests and united against each other. This was most evident militarily with the West's defence alliance NATO (founded in 1949) pitched against the Warsaw Pact (1955), the Soviet Union's military bloc.

This military integration not just bound together Western European nations as an exercise in promoting peace but also unified the bloc against a common enemy from the east. More importantly, it was a similar project (and a precursor) to Western Europe's economic integration.

Thus the great Schuman Declaration may have waxed lyrical about war and peace – but European integration came down to something as prosaic as coal and steel. What Schuman was really talking about was a treaty to pool coal and steel production – two of the most crucial industries in Europe.

Pooling Western Europe's coal and steel industries fulfilled two purposes at once. Applying the lessons learnt from 1871 and 1918 helped integrate the loser of World War II, Germany, instead of isolating it. It also

> *More than the genuine peace rhetoric after World War II, it was the Cold War, an ideological fear of communism, and economic profiteering that spurred Western European politicians to create the EU.*

gave shape to Western Europe's bloc-building exercise directed against the Soviet Union to form a strong alliance in the Cold War.

More than the genuine peace rhetoric after World War II, it was the Cold War, an ideological fear of communism, and economic profiteering that spurred Western European politicians to create the EU. After all, the EU has always been a project with an idealistic superstructure *and* a means of achieving less idealistic political goals. It has been a tool for overcoming nationalistic egotisms *and* a means of promoting national interests at the European level. It has been a framework for enabling trade between its members *and* a way of protecting one's own industries.

The dual nature of European integration is exemplified by the two core nations involved in the European project: Germany and France. Both subscribed to the narrative of promoting the project of European integration. But they did so for entirely different reasons.

For West Germany, European integration through the European Coal and Steel Community and the EEC was a pathway back to international recognition. The total defeat of Nazi Germany was not just a military collapse but a moral collapse as well. By its war atrocities and genocide of the Jews, Germany had turned itself into a pariah within the community of nations. It wanted to re-enter the international community, and closer economic and political engagement with its neighbours offered just that. Germany also needed this international engagement to reinstate the sovereignty it had lost to the Allied Forces of World War II (and would not finally regain them until the so-called 'two-plus-four' negotiations preceding Germany's reunification in 1990).

European integration was thus an insurance policy for France against both German and Soviet aggression.

Reaching out to its former arch enemy, Germany, made sense for France, too. In 1952, just a year after the European Coal and

Steel Community had been founded, Soviet leader Joseph Stalin proposed that Germany should be reunited and neutralised (the so-called 'Stalin Notes'). There was a real threat of the whole of Germany being drawn into the Soviet sphere of influence. France (and other Western countries) decided to counter Soviet advances by developing closer relations with West Germany and locking it into the Western sphere.

Second, spearheading the integration of Germany into Europe allowed France a degree of control over its former enemy. Metaphorically speaking, it was a close French embrace of Germany with the unvoiced intention of reducing the latter's ability to move. This motivation was visible in the European Coal and Steel Community, and it reared again in France's push for a European monetary union in the 1970s. The reasoning was simple: the more Germany was enmeshed in a European framework, the less it could dominate European affairs (and the greater would be France's influence).[8]

European integration was thus an insurance policy for France against both German and Soviet aggression. For Germany, European integration was a path back to respectability and sovereignty. But for either of them, it was unequivocally never solely a peace project (maybe not even predominantly).

None of this is to diminish the genuine efforts of European citizens of different countries to promote peace, reconciliation and international understanding. Of course, there were idealists driven by the desire to end war once and for all, and move towards a peaceful future for all of Europe. Out of this wish came countless initiatives such as student exchanges, town twinnings, and cultural cooperation.

Indeed, the past 70 years have been (largely) a time of peace for Europe. With the notable exceptions of the Balkan Wars of the 1990s and the current conflict between Russia and Ukraine, conflicts between states have not been allowed to escalate to the military level. The EU may claim that this is its own success, and it may be true to a degree. Having said that, the counterfactual is hard to prove. Would a Europe with NATO but without the EU have been less peaceful?

Regardless of whether and how much the EU can claim responsibility for post-War peace, there is a danger of falling prey to the European elite's rhetoric of integration as a peace project, which is used as a justification for all sorts of polices. For example, it was used to introduce the euro currency and bail out individual Eurozone members.

Calling the EU a by-product of the Cold War is a heresy in Europe, where the idealism of the European project is stressed at every occasion. But the louder the idealism, the more suspicious the public ought to be.

It is important to realise that Europe's integration was not just a peace project but also an exercise in power politics and economic profiteering. The role of the Cold War in creating the EU will otherwise be all too easily forgotten.

More importantly, accepting the real reasons behind the European project is essential to deal with Europe's current crisis of existence. European integration was not founded solely on idealism. But the pretence of such idealism often makes dealing with Europe's problems harder than it ought to be. If only we could discuss the euro crisis without having to put it in terms of war and peace, it would be easier to solve. Instead, European problems are addressed not in economic but in political terms.

It is high time to leave behind rose-tinted accounts of the history of European integration and approach it with a greater sense of realism.

BUILDING UTOPIA: EUROPE AS AN ELITIST PROJECT

The project of European integration embodied by the EU and its predecessors should not be confused with lofty idealism. It has been power politics from the moment it started. As such, it was initiated by those in power – and not by the governed. The entire framework of European integration has always been one designed by Europe's elites.

The peoples of Europe did not one day realise they wanted to be integrated and bound together by a supra-national organisation. The French, Italians or Dutch did not suddenly demand to be European henceforth. The Germans did not plead with their government to give up the Deutsche Mark and introduce the euro. There has never been a popular movement for any kind of European integration.

That European integration happened regardless is entirely due to the agenda of its political and economic elites. They convinced their people of the benefits of an integrated Europe – and if that was not enough, they were (and still are) prepared to go ahead with their agenda notwithstanding lack of popular support.

Eurobarometer results show how little the European project resonates with ordinary Europeans. Since 1973, the European Commission has been monitoring the evolution of public opinion in its member states. One of the regular questions is about popular interest in European affairs: "And as far as European politics are concerned, that is matters related to the European Community, to what extent would you say that you are interested in them?"

Figure 1 shows that mass interest in European politics was never particularly high. Perhaps alarmed by the prevalence of the answer "Not much" when people were asked about interest in EEC affairs, the Eurobarometer introduced a category "To some extent" in the mid-1980s. But even that did not improve the results much.

Figure 1: Eurobarometer on interest in European affairs

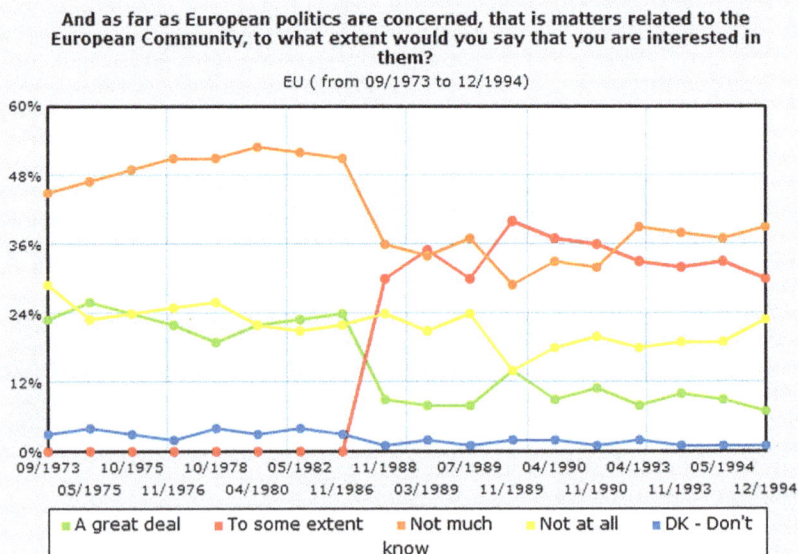

And as far as European politics are concerned, that is matters related to the European Community, to what extent would you say that you are interested in them?
EU (from 09/1973 to 12/1994)

"Great interest" in European affairs declined steadily. The predominant answers demonstrate that Europeans have had little interest in EEC affairs.

This lack of public interest corresponds with a lack of common knowledge about EU affairs. Paul Statham surveyed European journalists and asked them about their readers' interests. The answers were unequivocal: The interest and knowledge of national political affairs by far exceeded the corresponding figures at the EU level.[9]

Europe was never an issue high on people's agenda; nor was it something that would win the hearts and minds of ordinary Europeans. Most opinion polls show Europeans are lukewarm on European integration – not openly hostile, but certainly not glowing supporters either.

Europe was never an issue high on people's agenda; nor was it something that would win the hearts and minds of ordinary Europeans.

That the European integration project has proceeded despite such disinterest was only because European politicians kept pushing it – and are still pushing it.

A few examples easily demonstrate how elitist European integration has been. The first concerns the practice of seeking legitimacy for further European integration through referenda. This in itself is not elitist. On the contrary, it is only right and just that the peoples of Europe have a say in policymaking.

However, European referenda show their elitist streak the moment the people of Europe do not vote as the elites would like them to vote. When that happens, it does not mean the end of the matter. It typically means the referendum is either ignored – or the people get a second chance to come up with a "better" or "more correct" result.[10]

The first time this happened was when the Danes rejected the Maastricht Treaty in a 1992 referendum. Following this, the EU granted Denmark some concessions on the treaty, which justified putting an amended version to a second referendum a year later. This time it passed.

Ireland then rejected the Treaty of Nice in 2001 – only to be called back to the polls a year later. At their second chance, the Irish voted for the new treaty. History repeated itself when Ireland rejected the Treaty of Lisbon in 2008 – only to approve it a year later on the second chance.

Speaking of the Treaty of Lisbon, this treaty is in effect the planned and failed EU Constitution by another name.[11] But why did the Constitution fail? Because it was rejected not once but twice in referenda. Both France and the Netherlands threw it out in 2005. This should have killed the attempt to introduce the Constitution. Instead, the bulk of it was preserved and reintroduced under the Treaty of Lisbon – which, by the way, also meant that Britain did not hold a referendum on it. When it was still called the Constitution, all major British parties had pledged to put it to a referendum. Once it was renamed, the promise no longer applied.

Referenda that are held again and again if the first run does not produce the right result are one way in which Europe's elitist politicians work the system. An even more striking example are those referenda that are never held because politicians know they would fail.

The history of Europe's major treaties, such as the treaties of Rome, Maastricht, Nice or Lisbon, is one of treaties rarely ever being put to a popular vote. In the vast majority of countries, treaty changes are passed only by parliaments. Though theoretically that lends legitimacy to those treaties, it means rather than the electorate it is the very same political parties, whose leaders negotiate the treaties at the international stage, that pass them in national parliaments.

An additional complication is that political parties in some EU member states form a *de facto* cartel on EU matters. In the German Bundestag, for example, there is practically no opposition to fundamental EU matters (with the exception of a smallish post-communist party, The Left), while all other parties across the political spectrum support not just the EU project but also further integration. Political respectability, at least in Germany, required a subscription to the European integration consensus view. Questioning integration could turn any political party into a pariah. This means even if the public feels uneasy about EU affairs (or maybe is just not interested in them), such popular scepticism is not represented in parliament by their representatives.

Of course, politicians are only too aware of those areas of European integration that would never stand a chance of being implemented if the people were asked. Former German Chancellor Helmut Kohl, for example, has been very explicit in a number of interviews that he did not put the introduction of the euro currency to a popular vote because he knew it would have failed:

> *I knew that I could never win a referendum in Germany. We would have lost a referendum on the introduction of the euro. That's quite clear. I would have lost and by seven to three … If a Chancellor is trying to push something through, he must be a man of power. And if he's smart, he knows when the time is ripe. In one case – the euro – I was like a dictator.*[12]

If one were generous, one might call such behaviour political leadership. However, one might also be astounded by how a head of a democratically elected government knowingly put his own (elitist) views above the views of the vast majority of people.

Europe's elites, of course, would never accept the accusation of European elitism. They would rather maintain that Europe is a thoroughly democratic project – and to underline this assertion, they would point to the European Parliament, the parliament with second-largest electorate in the world (after India).

The European Parliament itself is not without its problems, though. Well, actually there are three. First, it is not a real parliament. Second, its democratic legitimacy evaporates a little bit more with each election. And third, the common European hardly takes any notice of it.

The first problem is the most basic one: Unlike national parliaments, the European Parliament does not have the right to initiate lawmaking procedures. This is not a triviality. Parliaments are often called legislatures because that is what they are there for: to legislate. The European Parliament can neither make laws on its own (it needs the European Commission, i.e. the executive branch of the EU, to do that), nor easily remove the executive (it needs a two-thirds majority). In effect, the European Parliament hardly deserves its name. It is a toothless parliament by the standards of most democratic nations.

Maybe because of the European Parliament's lack of power, few Europeans bother to vote in European elections – the second problem with European democracy. Since the first election to the European Parliament in 1979, voter turnout has decreased with every single election: from 63% in 1979 to just 42.5% in 2014.

Maybe because of the European Parliament's lack of power, few Europeans bother to vote in European elections...

The third problem with the European Parliament is loosely connected to the previous two: Europeans only really take notice of the European Parliament when it is elected every five years. And even then, turnout is low, and national rather than pan-European political topics dominate the election campaign. In between elections, the European Parliament hardly ever features in the media. It is no exaggeration to say that the vast majority of Europeans do not follow a single debate in the European Parliament in any given year. It is thus a Parliament that meets in splendid isolation from its voters – not entirely without function, admittedly, but almost entirely without a democratic audience. This is problematic not least because the European Parliament plays a crucial role in making laws affecting the entire EU – laws that may be highly unpopular if discussed at the national level. Once passed at the EU level, however, laws become binding, leaving little discretion for nation-states to deviate from them.

Despite its limited rights, low electoral turnout, and limited public reach, the European Parliament does not make the EU any less of an elitist project. On the contrary, EU parliamentarians are very much part of the EU elite.

From a democratic perspective, the state of European affairs is so dismal that it is often quipped that any country configured like the EU would struggle to be admitted into the EU. It would simply not be democratic enough to be worthy of accession.

Though this sounds like a harsh judgment, it is nevertheless true. EU affairs are and have always been deeply anti-democratic. It is a European elite that determines the course of European politics. This author has made his own experiences with what happens when the EU elite's view gets challenged (see Appendix 1).

In contrast, the will of the people does not matter. But then again, there is not a European people anyway but only European peoples – but that is a different problem altogether.

NO PEOPLE, NO COUNTRY

Of course there are some good things to be said about the EU. The common market is its greatest achievement. The four freedoms – the free movement of goods, persons, services and capital – have been almost fully realised. Great strides too have been made in unifying European markets, increasing competition, reducing transaction costs, and maximising consumer welfare.

The Schengen Agreement is another milestone for European integration. Being able to freely cross borders without controls from the North Cape to Sicily and from Lisbon to Warsaw has made travelling a remarkable experience. So much so that one forgets this was once a continent defined by borders that were often disputed, heavily controlled, and sometimes difficult to cross. And of course, with the caveats mentioned above, one could argue that the EU has made a contribution towards a more peaceful European order.

Despite such achievements, the EU's structural design flaws are at least in part responsible for some of the problems facing the union. The most fundamental is related to the lack of a European people.

What the EU seeks to achieve, it mainly does because it suits the interests of its individual member states but within the structure and institutions of a nation-state.

There is an executive government in the form of the European Commission. There is a legislature in the form of the European Parliament (deficient as it is), and there is a judiciary in the form of European courts in lieu of high courts or supreme courts.

There is only one problem with this. The institutions of a nation-state first and foremost require a nation. And for a true democracy to work, it needs a *demos* – a people. The EU does not have a people. No one self-identifies as purely or even mainly European (with the possible exception of the Germans still too ashamed to be German). Instead, the majority of Europeans self-identify as Czechs, French, Swedes or Italians, Maltese, Spanish and so on.

The institutions of a nation-state first and foremost require a nation.

Today, the 28 EU member states range from the tiny states of Luxembourg and Malta to industrial heavyweights like Germany and Italy, from formerly communist economies in Eastern Europe to the self-styled postmodern service economy of the United Kingdom.

The EU includes countries that are predominantly Protestant like Sweden and Catholic countries like Poland, as well as mainly atheist countries like the Czech Republic. It includes countries that have a civil law tradition like France and common law countries like Ireland. It includes countries with traditionally good fiscal discipline like Denmark and countries with large debt burdens like Greece.

In other words, the current EU is an assortment of 28 extremely diverse countries united under one banner. But the umbrella of EU membership has not eradicated the national peculiarities at all.

Least of all, the European project and the elites that have promoted it have not managed to form a European people, a *demos*, out of the many different nationalities. There is not even a pan-European identity to replace the national identities. But without a *demos*, can there ever be a true democracy?

Mark Steyn, the Canadian writer and commentator, summed up Europe's troubles when he said the core problem was that it was impossible to convince the Swedes that the Greeks were not foreigners to them, and *vice versa*. Though this may sounds flippant, it is indeed the fundamental problem.

Making the EU work requires overcoming the national and cultural differences within the continent. Desirable or not, for all practical purposes this task is impossible given Europe's extreme diversity.

EU structures are mimicking the workings of nation-states because the EU aspires to become supra-nation-state under its ultimate goal of "ever closer union". It is just not obvious how a single European people can ever be formed out of Europe's peoples.

PANEM ET CIRCENSES: THE RISE OF THE EUROPEAN WELFARE STATE

The anti-democratic political structures of European integration should have made the European project unpopular. Similarly, the declining relative importance of Europe should have been a concern for Europe's citizens. And if none of that bothered the Europeans, then maybe the slowing economic dynamism should have.

Yet despite such shortcomings, there have not been uprisings against (Western) Europe's status quo since World War II. European citizens witnessed falling average growth rates decade after decade. They saw mass unemployment become a persistent feature of their society. They also realised how their economies lost entire industries to newly developing countries. Despite this, there has been remarkable political stability for decades across the EU.

This is of course not to say that there have never been any changes of government, which sometimes even brought about some policy changes. However, the basic direction has remained the same. At least Western Europe countries were typically governed by parties that subscribed to a mixed economy model and continued with European integration through the EU and its predecessors. Whether governments were led by centre-left or centre-right parties or coalitions became a matter of aesthetic preference. It rarely ever mattered much beyond that.

Government spending as a percentage of GDP increased dramatically across Europe all through the 20th century (Table 1).

Table 1: Change in government spending as a percentage of GDP[13]

Country	Pre WWI (1913)	Post WWI (1920)	Pre WWII (1937)	1960	1990	2013
France	17.0	27.6	29.0	34.6	49.8	57.1
Germany	14.8	25.0	34.1	32.4	45.1	44.3
Italy	17.1	30.1	31.1	30.1	53.4	50.5
UK	12.7	26.2	30.0	32.2	39.9	46.9
Belgium	13.8	22.1	21.8	30.3	54.3	54.7
Netherlands	9.0	13.5	19.0	33.7	54.1	49.8
Spain	11.0	8.3	13.2	18.8	50.1	44.3

The pattern of government growth is also similar across Europe. Both world wars increased government spending (except in Spain, which remained neutral in World War I and thus did not have to increase its expenditure). Since the immediate post-World War II and reconstruction era, government spending has increased to unprecedented levels. The most extreme case is France where the state now accounts for well over half of the economy.

These spending rises have not been driven by the core areas of government spending of law and order, defence and certain public goods. Instead, all the increases in government spending have been in education, health and welfare.

In a 2014 paper for the Centre for Policy Studies, economist Brian Sturgess analysed data for 19 European OECD countries for 15 years from 1996 to 2011. He found that on average, European governments now direct only 19% of their total spending to core responsibilities, while 10% is spent on subsidies and infrastructure, 12% on education, 15% on health, and 38% on social security.[14]

On average, these European countries spent almost 30% of GDP on welfare alone, which is more than the total of government spending before World War II.

There are many possible explanations for this growth of government. American economist Robert Higgs describes a ratchet effect in his book *Crisis and Leviathan*. In times of real or imagined national emergencies, mainly wars and recessions, government takes over previously private rights and activities. When the crisis passes, government retreats somewhat, but never to the same level as before.[15] This ratchet effect could indeed explain why European governments increased in size during the two world wars. However, it is less well suited to explain the additional (and substantial) government growth since 1945.

Another explanation is the rise of Keynesian economics after World War II. Keynesian demand-side management had given governments a licence to increase spending to 'stimulate' the economy. This probably contributed somewhat to the growth of government. However, not every European country subscribed to Keynesian policies. Germany, for example, only briefly flirted with Keynesianism in the late 1960s and 1970s, and yet its spending record was similar to that of countries where Keynesianism was stronger.

The theory of public choice explains this growth in government spending as a consequence of lobby activities and rent seeking. Public choice undoubtedly has strong explanatory power – but it still does not explain why European governments grew much faster than their counterparts in other developed economies such as the US, Australia or New Zealand.

Perhaps the burgeoning size of government in Europe has something to do with the specific political structure of the EU. Though this argument might be hard to prove empirically, there is some value to it. In building the unpopular political superstructure of the EU, the European elites had to ensure the electorate would not desert them. They achieved this by establishing a welfare state that went far beyond a mere safety net. Instead, European welfare states became an all-encompassing insurance and entertainment scheme.

Seen this way, the European welfare state was a means of buying the public's silence and acquiescence. It was the same method of securing power Juvenal described in his *Satires* two millennia ago:

Bread and circuses – or *panem et circenses* in the Latin original – were the means of bribing the masses in ancient Rome. Modern Europe is witnessing a similar phenomenon. To their subservient citizens, the European elites provide free or heavily subsidised education, health care, TV and radio programmes, roads, income support and pensions, public transport, libraries, opera houses, and theatres.

Unfortunately, it is often overlooked that government can only bribe the people with their own money. In the words of the great French economist Frédéric Bastiat: "Government is the great fiction through which everybody endeavours to live at the expense of everybody else."

As a result, the very people benefiting from the welfare state are also footing the bill – at an astonishing cost. Last year, the German Federation of Taxpayers calculated the difference between gross wages and net take-home pay based on OECD data. To do this, they also included the effect of value added taxes, which are often hidden from view.[16]

For a single income earner on the national average income, Belgium topped the list of predatory governments with a tax burden of 59.1%, followed by Hungary (54%) and Germany (53.1%). In most large European economies, the burden was well above 40%.

The respective tax burdens for families with two income earners and two children are somewhat lower, but tax burdens in Europe still range from 47% in Greece to 29.4% in the UK. By comparison, the figures for Australia and New Zealand 23.2% and 15.5%, respectively.

Buying European citizens' loyalty for their mixed economy welfare states has effectively enslaved them. Is that the price of peace the EU claims it has brought to the continent? Has Europe lost its economic liberty as the price of national safety?

The welfare state (broadly defined as all government spending outside the state's core functions) was the means by which Europe bought itself political stability. Little wonder, then, that the moment governments could no longer afford to pay for it, the previous political consensus started falling apart. This also explains the rise of radical parties such as SYRIZA in Greece, the National Front in France, and Podemos in Spain.

The rise of the European welfare state, the reduction of economic dynamism, and the increasingly questionable legitimacy of the European project go hand in hand. *Panem et circenses* could have been the motto of Europe's post-World War II mixed economy model. It remains to be seen whether the EU will also share the Roman Empire's fate.

EUROPE'S DEMOGRAPHIC TIME BOMB

Europe's political and economic problems will soon be exacerbated by its ageing society. In a number of European countries, birth rates have been very low for several decades. The replacement fertility rate, that is, the fertility rate at which populations would remain constant over time, is 2.1. That means if women have, on average, 2.1 children over their lifetime, then every generation would be replaced by a new generation of the same size.

The current average fertility rate for the EU, however, stands at just 1.58. This means the next generation will be about a quarter smaller than the current generation. If the trend continues, this new generation will be succeeded by another generation that is another 25% smaller.

Combine this drop in fertility with improvements in life expectancy and the result is a rapidly ageing society. The current median age of 45 years in Germany and Italy will reach 50 years by the middle of the century. At the same time, working age populations will collapse. Over the next four decades, Germany will lose about a third of its working age population. These trends are present in varying degrees in most European countries.

An older population not only means more pensioners but also rapidly increasing health costs. Given the already precarious state of public finances across Europe, the continent will struggle to shoulder these burdens. Population ageing and shrinking will also mean that Europe can expect subdued economic growth rates for decades to come.

Some experts argue that immigration could be used to correct this demographic imbalance. Unfortunately, the scale of the problem is far too great for migration to fix. Just to maintain its current workforce-to-retiree ratio, Europe would need an influx of migrants several times above its current intake. Such an unprecedented increase is not politically viable, though. Immigration is already one of the most contentious issues in European politics – not least because Europe has never been particularly good at attracting skilled migrants, let alone integrating those migrants it got.

Population ageing and shrinking as well as falling fertility rates are problems in most European countries. Why the fertility rate collapsed as much as it has is a matter for debate. Cultural pessimists like Theodore Dalrymple argue that modern European society values its material standard of living more highly than anything else. Children are only "obstructions to the enjoyment of life, a drain on resources, an obstacle to next year's holiday in Bali or wherever it might be", he writes in his book *The New Vichy Syndrome*.

But whatever its reasons, the main problem with demographic change is its sluggish nature. A development that has been going in the wrong direction for 25 years takes 75 years to correct. There is no quick fix for demographic faults; the skid marks of demographic change are too deep and too long.

Even if Europe somehow managed to improve the situation of its younger generation and boost fertility rates to more sustainable levels, it cannot hold off the process of ageing and shrinking for a few more decades. The potential mothers to give birth to a new and stronger generation of Europeans have not been born themselves.

The consequences of these demographic changes will be severe. It will be difficult for European nations to service their debt, let alone repay it, with both shrinking and ageing populations. There is only so much that increased productivity can do to compensate for a collapsing workforce.

And then there is the psychological effect. Older societies may be more peaceful than younger ones. But they are also less creative, less dynamic, and more risk averse. Europe will possibly become a less entrepreneurial place in the future. When more than half the population is over the age of 50, how likely is it that the next big technological innovation will emerge in such a social climate?

THE EURO FALLACY

A discussion of Europe's problems would not be complete without a look at the failings of Europe's monetary union. When we talk about the euro crisis today, we immediately think of Greece, which has been on the brink of default since late 2009. However, the euro crisis is not just a crisis of Greece.

In Europe's monetary union are all the hallmarks of Europe's integration failings. Monetary union was a project designed by Europe's elites against the wishes of their peoples. It was a political power play designed to weaken Germany (only to see it strengthened). Finally, it was an undertaking that has damaged Europe's economy and competitiveness.

To understand how Europe's monetary union happened, it is worthwhile to remember what Europe looked like before the introduction of the euro. There had always been structural differences between Europe's economies. Before the euro, such differences in competitiveness were reflected in long-term adjustments in exchange rates. However, such devaluations were considered a sign of weakness and a national embarrassment, and were unpopular in the countries that had to devalue.

Consider this: In the 35 years before the introduction of the euro, all major European currencies progressively lost value against the Deutsche Mark. In 1963, DM81.36 could buy 100 French francs compared to only DM29.82 on the eve of the euro's introduction on 1 January 1999 – a devaluation of 63.3%.

It was even more extreme for the Italian lira. In 1963, 1,000 lire cost DM6.41 compared to only DM1.01 in 1998 – in other words, the lira had lost 84.2% of its value against the Deutsche Mark.

Similar developments occurred against the Greek drachma, the Portuguese escudo, the Spanish peseta, and other currencies.

If the monetary union did not work well before the euro crisis, it is even worse now.

The massive devaluations of other currencies against the German Mark indicate the very tight monetary policy of the old German Bundesbank and the high competitiveness and productivity of the German economy compared to the rest of Europe.

European economies like Italy, Spain and France thus regularly devalued their currency to remain competitive with Germany. It was humiliating for the French, the Spanish and the Italians – the very reason they had pushed Germany into monetary union back-fired spectacularly on them.

Germany had resisted monetary union since it was first proposed in the 1970s. However, it needed the support of its neighbours for its reunification project after the Fall of the Berlin Wall in 1989, and France used this leverage to push Germany to relinquish the Deutsche Mark and adopt the euro.

Germany's unification was a diplomatic balancing act, which played out in the 'two-plus-four' negotiations (between the two German states and the four allied forces – Britain, France, the Soviet Union and the US) that paved the way for Germany's reunification in October 1990.

It was difficult to reunite Germany – not least because the British and the French had to be reassured that they had nothing to fear from this new and bigger country in the heart of Europe.

British Prime Minister Margaret Thatcher was horrified at the prospect of a united Germany. "We beat the Germans twice, and now they're back," she allegedly told a meeting of European leaders at the time.[19]

Thatcher even invited historians to a seminar at Chequers to discuss how dangerous the Germans really were. Her trade minister, Nicholas Ridley, was forced to resign after he compared German Chancellor Helmut Kohl to Adolf Hitler in an interview with *The Spectator*.

French suspicions of the rise of a new evil German superstate were equally strong, as previously confidential memos released by the British Foreign Office reveal. President François Mitterrand was convinced that the prospect of unification had turned the Germans into the 'bad Germans' they used to be. He saw them as behaving brutally in pursuit of their new national interests, thereby upsetting the political and security settings of Europe. In a conversation with then US President George H.W. Bush, Mitterrand remarked, "I like Germany so much I think there should be two of them!"

Tensions were deep between Germany and its neighbours around the time of reunification. Even the Soviet Union was more open to the idea than West Germany's old allies. France especially needed to be convinced that it had nothing to fear from a reunited Germany.

There had always been rumours that in the 'two-plus-four' negotiations, the French had demanded Germany to give up its beloved Deutsche Mark in return for a French 'oui' on reunification. More than once, the dominance of the über-solid Deutsche Mark had caused the French and other European nations pain. Forcing the Germans to abandon their currency was thus an appropriate way to weaken them so they could not become a threat to other nations, the French probably thought.

Then World Bank President Robert Zoellick, who was the US lead negotiator in the 'two-plus-four' negotiations, confirmed in 2011 that France had demanded the Germans sacrifice the Deutsche Mark. According to Zoellick, the euro currency is a by-product of German reunification and was meant to calm Mitterrand's fears of an all-too-powerful Germany.[20]

The great historical irony of this story is, of course, that if the French had really planned to weaken the powers of the newly reunited Germany through monetary union, the plan completely backfired. In strategic terms, Germany's influence has never been greater. With the continent relying on Germany's AAA rating, Berlin can now effectively dictate fiscal policy to Athens, Lisbon and Rome – perhaps in the future to Paris, too. This was most definitely not what Mitterrand had planned.

Perhaps an even greater irony is that the Germans are not at all happy with their new hegemonic power within Europe. As opinion polls show, they have not the slightest interest in ruling the European periphery. In fact, the Germans would be content being just a bigger version of Switzerland – prosperous, a bit boring, and vigorously unengaged in international affairs. It is the very role the West Germans learnt to play to perfection between 1945 and 1990. This also means France and Britain had nothing to fear from the Germans at the time of reunification. If they had known the post-war Germans better, they would have been more relaxed about a larger Germany.

As it turns out, the euro started as a French insurance policy against German power. But even as an insurance policy it has failed. Instead, it has turned the Germans against their will into the new rulers of Europe. And it has consigned France to be the weaker partner in the Franco-German relationship.

European monetary union thus has a colourful political history but it has failed to weaken Germany's economic influence. Unfortunately, that is not the euro's only failure – far from it.

The euro crisis is now more than five years old. It was in late 2009 when then Greek Prime Minister George Papandreou admitted that his country had a fiscal problem. Many now see this as the beginning of the euro crisis.

The truth is the crisis started much earlier – namely on the day the euro was introduced, first as an electronic currency in 1999 and then as coins and paper in 2002.

To see why the euro was in crisis even then, when many politicians still claim that all was well before the global financial crisis, one needs to look behind the façade of monetary union. It is true that before 2009, few people spoke of a euro crisis, yields on government debt were low, and the exchange rate of the euro was by and large stable. But beneath this seeming stability, something was clearly wrong in European monetary and economic affairs.

The first problem was the divergence in competitiveness, which started immediately after the euro was introduced. Where previously such competitiveness differences would have resulted in exchange rate adjustments, they now resulted in diverging unit labour costs. Put simply, German products became cheaper on the world market, whereas, say, Italian or Portuguese products became more expensive.

The introduction of the euro had kept a lid on wage increases across the German economy because Germany had entered the EU with a too high exchange rate. This led to high unemployment in Germany, followed by dramatic economic reforms, especially of its labour market, and a policy of wage restraint. Both the wage restraint and economic reforms were painful, but combined they ensured Germany became more and more productive and competitive over time. Unit labour costs fell substantially in Germany.

Meanwhile, the southern European economies, who had entered monetary union with the competitive advantage of low exchange rates, enjoyed a sudden economic boom made possible by lower interest rates than they had previously known.

However, the chronic inability of southern European countries to implement the kind of tough economic reforms Germany had meant that countries such as Greece, Spain and Portugal slipped further down the European competitiveness ladder. Their products became more expensive, and their governments more indebted. The consequences were substantial deficits in the current account and high unemployment in countries with excessive wage increases.

But these competitiveness developments were not the only thing wrong with the euro. The euro's official interest rate reflected the circumstances of a struggling Germany but not the boom in periphery countries.

The unrestrained building boom in Spain and Ireland was bound to end in a fiasco. The collapse of the construction sector not only triggered a rapid rise in unemployment but also plunged the banking sector, faced with huge write-offs on related real estate lending, into a deep crisis – with devastating effects on the fiscal situation.

Finally, the euro also failed to impose fiscal discipline on its member countries, so nobody played by the rules that were supposed to govern the monetary union. No country was supposed to enter the EU with debts of more than 60% of GDP – yet Belgium, Italy and Greece did. No EU country was supposed to run deficits higher than 3% of GDP – yet France and Germany did in 2003/04 without being punished.

The political independence of the European Central Bank (ECB) was also damaged right from the start. Its first president, Wim Duisenberg from the Netherlands, had been elected for a full eight-year term. However, political pressure from the French government forced him to resign his position after four years to allow his colleague Jean-Claude Trichet to take over.

Take these three issues together – diverging competitiveness, property bubbles in the periphery, and a misgoverned Eurozone – and it is clear the EU was dysfunctional much before the global financial crisis. In fact, the crisis acted as a catalyst to alert markets to rethink risk – and when they took a closer look at Europe they realised the mess it was in.

If the monetary union did not work well before the euro crisis, it is even worse now.

Since the euro crisis erupted around 2009/10, Europe has witnessed years of bungled crisis management, explicit and covert bailouts, and imposed austerity budgets to enforce 'internal devaluation'. None of these have managed to end the crisis.

The only thing that has slowed down somewhat is the acute market panic over Europe – but only because markets have become used to a constant flow of bad news from Europe. Europe's crisis is the new normal, and everybody seems to be accepting it. At least, European policymakers are doing so by proclaiming current policies to be "without alternative".

It was a mistake to introduce the euro before Europe was ready for it. But it is an even bigger mistake to pretend that this badly designed monetary union must be defended at all cost. It would be far better for the Europeans to cut their losses and give up on the euro.

If Europe continues with its current policies, the result will be disastrous for everyone involved. Forcing crisis countries to continue devaluing internally by cutting wages, pensions and prices will increase their already high unemployment rates. It will condemn their young generations to misery and destabilise their political systems – and there is no guarantee that this recipe would ultimately improve their economic fortunes and make their products competitive internationally. Meanwhile, the financial commitments of those countries underwriting the bailout guarantees will eventually exceed their ability, let alone their willingness, to pay for their neighbours' economic mismanagement.

Of course, any exit path from the monetary union will be painful for all. But at least there will be hope that once Europe's countries return to currencies suited to their respective economy, they would be able to generate growth and employment. Breaking up the Eurozone would also help deal with the persistent trade imbalances in Europe, help crisis countries to export more, and make stronger economies such as Germany import more. It would also create a badly needed mechanism of exchange rate flexibility between European countries.

Although the end of the euro's reign and a return to national currencies may be good economics, it is highly unlikely to happen. Europe's leaders would lose face if, after decades of propagating the benefits of monetary union, they allowed a new monetary diversity of Europe – as desirable as it may be.

So what's going to happen next? Is there another solution at all?

Unfortunately, there is no positive solution in sight. Most likely, the ECB will inflate the problems away.

The ECB has been intervening in bond markets since the beginning of the euro crisis, and even more so with its 'quantitative easing' programme in early 2015. It is no doubt due to such interventions that the euro is still alive.

This is an utterly absurd situation. Bailing out other countries (and their banks), pooling Europe's sovereign debt, or issuing Eurobonds may be incompatible with the German Constitution. Such tactics may well violate EU treaty law. They lack any meaningful democratic legitimacy. They are certainly unpopular in those countries most likely to foot the bill.

In theory, such measures should be impossible to implement.

But disguised as monetary policy, these quintessentially fiscal arrangements not only become possible, but they almost look legal. Simply claiming that the monetary transmission mechanism is broken is used as sufficient justification to save the whole of Europe from bankruptcy.

Even better is that while fiscal measures are necessarily limited to the funds countries can raise in taxes or through running deficits, monetary interventions in a fiat money world have no such limitations. They can run for as long as tree trunks can be turned into paper money or zeros added to electronic accounts.

But perhaps the biggest 'advantage' of Europe's current malaise is that not a single national parliament needs to be consulted before the ECB finally opens the floodgates. No European government needs to be involved in the process, and even if opposed to the measures, parliaments and governments have no realistic chance of stopping them.

Of course there is a lot to be said for central bank independence. In the case of the ECB, however, one may well wonder whether its actions are still covered by its independence in monetary affairs or, indeed, whether the ECB has moved into the terrain of fiscal policy for which it is not responsible.

The way Europe is dealing with the crisis of its monetary union is exactly the way it has always dealt with its challenges: in the most undemocratic way imaginable (see also Appendix 2 for an account of the international crisis management around Greece since 2010).

Whether this will be enough to save the euro in the long run is nevertheless a different question. It is often said that if something cannot go on forever, it will stop. The euro is such a thing. It cannot go on forever, and so it will eventually fail. In fact, it would and should have failed already because of its inherent weaknesses. The only reason it is still with us is the political support it still enjoys. But even such political support may turn out to be a weak life insurance.

EUROPEAN LESSONS FOR NEW ZEALAND

This essay was meant to draw a rough sketch of Europe's current problems and put the grand European integration experiment into its historical context. In doing so, it discussed the result of a power play in European politics that started during the Cold War and embraced Germany to control it.

But the European integration project always suffered from an inherent flaw. There never was a European *demos* to drive the political and economic integration. European integration has always been a top-down, elite driven project. National interests have not been superseded by a European vision. On the contrary, national interests and egotisms are still alive in Europe. Though this integration project has never been too popular with ordinary voters, any dissent has been sedated by the stunning growth of the welfare state.

Despite these shortcomings, the EU has achievements to be proud of. The biggest one is the creation of a common market in which people, goods, capital and services can cross borders easily. The Schengen Agreement allowing for passport-free travel across the continent is another success. A once war-torn continent has been politically stable and strife free for 70 years.

But Europe is also battling socio-economic realities on many fronts. Its governments are heavily indebted, and its populations are ageing and shrinking. The euro crisis has brought many of Europe's previously hidden economic problems to the fore.

For us in this part of the world, the tyranny of distance from Europe has finally turned into a blessing. Now we have to make sure we do not repeat Europe's mistakes. But what are those European mistakes that can be avoided in New Zealand? And what are the lessons we can learn from Europe's integration disaster?

Fortunately, there are some elements of the European experience that will never have an equivalent in a New Zealand context. New Zealand's geographic isolation means it will not enter into any arrangements that will undermine its sovereignty and democracy as a nation-state. The only exception is its special relationship with Australia, which has become more integrated over the past three decades of Closer Economic Relations. But even in New Zealand's relationship with Australia, integration is unlikely ever to pass the threshold of shared political institutions or monetary union (even though it used to be discussed in the past).

Seen from the outside, the degree to which European affairs are not controlled by the peoples of Europe but by a narrow political elite is shocking.

New Zealand should nevertheless pay close attention to two aspects of the developments in Europe. First, the way in which elites have captured the political decision-making process should be avoided here. Second, the rise of the European welfare state is a cautionary example.

Seen from the outside, the degree to which European affairs are not controlled by the peoples of Europe but by a narrow political elite is shocking. European voters are not presented with a clear choice on the course of European integration.

One should be careful not to equate democracy with good governance, the rule of law, or even individual liberty. Having said that, a well-functioning democracy can support all of these goals. Europe's democracy, however, can only be called deficient. European integration meant that an extra level of decision-making has been placed between Europe's citizens and their leaders. Ordinary Europeans are far removed from the most important decisions affecting their continent. They have no direct or meaningful say on issues such as Europe's monetary union, agricultural policy, or foreign relations. There are simply no elections that would be fought over such issues.

New Zealand would do well to avoid letting its political elites from becoming as distant from voters. In a small country such as ours, this temptation may be easier to resist than in a densely populated continent such as Europe. But it is not just size that matters but attitude. Europe's leaders have shown an elitist streak that we should never let any politician get away with in New Zealand.

The more we can strengthen the connection between citizens and their representatives, or rather citizens and political decision-making, the better. This means more elements of direct democracy and greater devolution of political power to the community and local government. Seen in this light, the creation of the Auckland super city and further attempts to amalgamate councils are all steps in the wrong direction. They remove government from the people it is supposed to serve. Europe's first lesson is to distrust the distant political elites.

The second lesson is to be watchful of the rise of the welfare state. In Europe, the welfare state was a means of buying political power. Of course, the bribed electorate always paid for its own bribes. However, the arrangement worked for as long as new spending commitments could be financed through higher taxes, more debt, or indeed a combination of both. As government spending has now reached around 50% of GDP, and as the debt load stands at worrying levels, the European welfare state model has reached its limits. Europe's demographic change will make it even harder to maintain the welfare state in the future.

New Zealand needs to avoid a replay of this 'welfare state and debt' disaster. Fortunately, our own spending and debt levels are substantially below Europe's. But our society will age too, and there is always a temptation for politicians to buy their way to power through the welfare state. Europe shows where such policies can lead to.

In their report *Guarding the Public Purse*, Bryce Wilkinson and Khyaati Acharya have shown how demographic change will affect New Zealand's public finances over the coming decades. One of their observations was that under current policies, government spending on social welfare, including health and education, was projected to rise from 24.6% to 28.2% of GDP between 2011 and 2061, due to ageing alone.[21] This would move New Zealand to levels currently experienced in Europe.

In New Zealand we have the luxury of being three or four decades behind Europe's demography curve. But this does not have to mean that we will be experiencing Europe's problems 30 or 40 years later. It should mean that we have 30 or 40 years of finding ways to prevent a European replay by finding different answers to the challenges facing Europe today.

CONCLUSION

The standout reasons for Europe's decline are its elitist political system and its inflated welfare state – and the interrelations between these two.

Europe no longer rules the world. Nor can it hope to regain the dominant position it once enjoyed. Europe's decline is entirely self-inflicted. It is a continent that first destroyed itself in two world wars. It then weakened itself by inflating the activities of the state while creating a bureaucratic, isolated, and elitist superstructure in the form of the EU. It also wrecked its monetary system by introducing a common currency that was never going to work and caused more problems than it ever solved.

In many ways, Europe is a case study in how not to conduct one's economic and political affairs, which makes it all the more worthwhile to pay attention to European affairs so we do not repeat their mistakes here. But don't hold your breath. Short-term political gains through welfare spending is too tempting for politicians anywhere and too beguiling for voters.

ENDNOTES

1 The Maddison-Project, http://www.ggdc.net/maddison/maddison-project/home.htm, 2013 version.

2 IMF, World Economic Outlook (October 2013), database.

3 World Population Prospects: The 2012 Revision, Population Division of the Department of Economic and Social Affairs of the United Nations Secretariat (June 2013), http://esa.un.org/wpp/Excel-Data/EXCEL_FILES/1_Population/WPP2012_POP_F01_1_TOTAL_POPULATION_BOTH_SEXES.XLS.

4 "Does Europe account for half of the world's welfare spending?" Full Fact (16 January 2014), https://fullfact.org/factchecks/europe_half_world_welfare_spending-29324.

5 European Union, "The Schuman Declaration – 9 May 1950," http://europa.eu/about-eu/basic-information/symbols/europe-day/schuman-declaration/index_en.htm.

6 Joe Murphy, "Peace in Europe at risk: Dire warning from German leader Merkel," *Evening Standard* (London: 26 October 2011), http://www.standdard.co.uk/news/peace-in-europe-at-risk-dire-warning-from-german-leader-merkel-6361270.html.

7 European Union, "The Founding Fathers of the EU," http://europa.eu/about-eu/eu-history/founding-fathers/index_en.htm.

8 For an account of the origins of the euro, see Johan van Overtveldt, *The End of the Euro: The Uneasy Future of the European Union* (Chicago: B2 Books, 2011).

9 Paul Statham, "Making Europe News: Journalism and Media Performance," in Ruud Koopmans and Paul Statham (eds), *The Making of a European Public Sphere: Media Discourse and Political Contention* (Cambridge (Mass.): Cambridge University Press, 2010), p. 131.

10 Gráinne de Búrca, "If at First You Don't Succeed: Vote, Vote Again: Analyzing the Second Referendum Phenomenon in EU Treaty Change," *Fordham International Law Journal* 33:5 (2011), pp. 1472–1489.

11 Bruno Waterfield, "Lisbon Treaty resurrects the defeated EU Constitution," *The Daily Telegraph* (London: 13 June 2008).

12 Jeevan Vasagar, "Helmut Kohl: I acted like a dictator to bring in the euro,"*The Daily Telegraph* (London: 9 April 2013).

13 Vito Tanzi, "The Economic Role of the State in the 21st Century," *Cato Journal* 25:3 (Fall 2005), pp. 617–638. 2013 data sourced from http://www.tradingeconomics.com/germany/government-spending-to-gdp.

14 Brian Sturgess, *Not Paved With Gold: Government 'Investment' Does Not Equal Growth* (London: Centre for Policy Studies, 2014).

15 Robert Higgs, *Crisis and Leviathan: Critical Episodes in the Growth of American Government* (New York: Oxford University Press, 1987).

16 Volker Stern, *Rundschreiben 8/2014: Zum Steuerzahlergedenktag 2013 und 2014* (Berlin: Deutsches Steuerzahlerinstitut des Bundes der Steuerzahler, 2014), http://www.steuerzahler.de/files/61647/RS_08-2014_-_Stern_-_Zum_Steuerzahlergedenktag_2013_und_2014.pdf.

17 Eurostat, Fertility Statistics, http://ec.europa.eu/eurostat/statistics-explained/index.php/Fertility_statistics.

[18] Oliver Hartwich, *Selection, Migration and Integration: Why Multiculturalism Works in Australia (And Fails in Europe)*, Sydney: The Centre for Independent Studies, 2011.

[19] Carsten Volkery, "The Iron Lady's views on German reunification: 'The Germans are back!'," *Spiegel Online* (11 September 2009), http://www. spiegel.de/international/europe/the-iron-lady-s-views-on-german-reunification-the-germans-are-back-a-648364. html.

[20] Oliver Hartwich, "A euro power play that backfired," *Business Spectator* (17 August 2011), http://www.businessspectator.com. au/bs.nsf/Article/France-Germany-euro-currency-debt-crisis-markets-r-pd20110816-KS5LK?OpenDocument.

[21] Bryce Wilkinson and Khyaati Acharya, *Guarding the Public Purse*, Wellington: The New Zealand Initiative, 2014.

PAYING DEARLY FOR EUROPEAN INSANITY

Europe's political elites are gathered in Brussels today for yet another emergency summit on the euro currency. For this column it would be tempting to seize the moment and rehash all the arguments for why the euro will never work and cannot be saved.

But after almost two years of the euro crisis, even I am getting tired of this exercise. And in a way, at least outside EU circles, everybody knows why the common currency is doomed. So instead let me reflect on the underlying psychological flaws of European policymaking.

Einstein once defined insanity as, "doing the same thing over and over again and expecting different results." He must have had the European Union in mind.

Bailing out one country after the other, Europe's leaders never tire to claim that this last bailout, this last emergency summit, this last rescue mechanism will finally solve the crisis once and for all. And then, two weeks later, they are meeting again to proclaim exactly the same after another emergency round. The motto of Europe's crisis management is always 'this time is different'.

Clearly, in the Einsteinian sense, European politicians are insane. They are unwilling to learn the lessons of their dilettantism because that would require admitting previous failures.

There is a general European unwillingness to accept criticism. Nothing that deviates from the EU's own narrative about the inevitability of ever closer union is allowed to spoil the party. How else could one understand German treasurer Wolfgang Schäuble? Last week he seriously claimed that the euro was a 'success story' and that it had especially benefitted countries like Greece. In psychology, they have a term for such pathological behaviour. It's called denial.

I have my very own experiences with European denialism and the EU's unwillingness to take criticism. As a high school student in Germany, more than twenty years ago, I took part in the 'Europe at School' essay competition. Every year since 1953 students have been encouraged to write essays on questions of European integration.

When I submitted a critical piece on European politics one year, I won a small consolation prize. The next year, the topic allowed for a slightly more optimistic assessment and so I gained an invitation from the speaker of parliament to Bonn. However, when another year later I wholeheartedly praised the beneficial effects of the Single Market I was awarded with the Honorary Prize of the Federal Chancellor. I still have the big book prize with the handwritten personal dedication from Helmut Kohl on my shelves at home.

It was very obvious how the competition worked. The more you applauded the EU, the more the judges liked your essays. It all had a whiff of Soviet-style indoctrination. If only I had learnt my lessons at school I would still be writing panegyrics on the EU today. But that would have meant turning a blind eye to the serious flaws of the EU project.

Not much has changed since my high school days, as I discovered last week. I had been invited to deliver a public lecture to the Centre for European Studies at the Australian National University, an institution part-funded by the EU.

The title of my speech, 'Europe's painful farewell', had obviously made the delegation of the EU Commission in Canberra nervous. Perhaps they also keep a file with all my incriminating Business Spectator columns on Europe. In any case, two weeks before the event I was informed that they would send their First Counsellor to formally respond to my speech. It was undoubtedly an exercise in limiting the damage from my EU-sceptical views.

As I heard from a reliable source, the EU delegation was deeply concerned about the things I had to say. And so in order to neutralise my outrageous opinions European embassies were asked to ensure their diplomats attended the event as well. They did.

Apart from a handful of Australians, last Wednesday's audience at ANU was a small assembly of European diplomats. They came from countries like France, Germany, Belgium, Denmark, Finland and Malta. Even Croatia, not yet part of the European Union, had sent a representative. The things you need to do to become an EU member.

After I had finished my speech on the sad state of Europe, it happened as I had expected. One EU diplomat after the other rose to sing the praises of the EU and defend it against all criticisms, even those I had not made. They were so passionate in their speeches that I wondered whether the EU delegation had offered a prize for the best defence of the EU. Perhaps they could win a romantic dinner with either EU foreign secretary Catherine Ashton or EU president Herman van Rompuy?

In any case, it was telling that none of the diplomats even bothered to respond to my economic concerns about Europe's debt and monetary crisis. Instead, one after the other began their statements with variations of 'I'm not an economist but …'

And so I was informed that soon Europe would lead the world in green technologies, the euro was an important symbol of integration, and small hiccups like the debt crisis would not deter the EU from pursuing its integration agenda further. Their refusal to engage with my criticism on an economic basis was so bizarre that I'd rather not try to imagine how it must have sounded to the few Australians in the room.

A day later I received an email from one of the European embassies in Canberra. Writing in an apologetic tone, a senior diplomat who had attended the event told me that he was grateful for my views. Later I also spoke with another friendly European diplomat. He asked me not to take his colleagues' public utterances too seriously. "They're only doing their jobs; of course we all know what a terrible state Europe is in."

Everything that's wrong with Europe, it was on display in Canberra last week. Economic questions are treated as political ones; high hopes have to pass as strategies; utopias are considered realities. And if you harbour any doubts about whether all of this makes sense you better keep them to yourself. For otherwise you leave the sphere of what is officially sanctioned as respectable and politically correct politics.

If this were only a problem for Europe, the EU's denialism would be bad enough. But it isn't. The refusal of EU elites to come to grips with their failures is the biggest threat to the global economy. The world will pay dearly for Europe's stubborn utopianism.

Published in Business Spectator (Melbourne), 21 July 2011.
Reproduced with permission.

THE EUROZONE MUST STOP PLAYING THE BLAME GAME

Okay, my dear *Business Spectator* readers. For the past five years I have been trying to deliver you balanced and well-researched columns, with the odd provocation thrown in for entertainment. Today, on day one after the Greek default, I just cannot do that. Because I am angry.

So with apologies to you and the fantastic *Business Spectator* editors, here is my Athens rant.

The past week must have been the most extraordinary yet in the neverending euro crisis. I just cannot recall anything like it ever happening before. What we have witnessed is an incredible combination of political dilettantism, chutzpah and aggression.

No-one in this euro game is innocent. Everyone involved has to take their share of the blame and acknowledge their roles in the escalating crisis.

To start with the original sin of the euro crisis, Greece should have never, ever been made a part of the eurozone. And the eurozone should have never happened in the first place.

The whole idea of uniting vastly different European economies under one currency, one interest rate and one exchange was not just folly; it was madness. It had nothing to do with economics because it was so obviously not an optimum currency area; it was always just about political power.

If Germany had not needed France's approval for re-unification in 1990, the Germans would have never given up their deutschemark voluntarily. But that was the price they had to pay for France accepting a bigger neighbour to the east. The French thought that binding Germany into the corset of a monetary union would curb her power. What a colossal miscalculation.

The next grave mistake was admitting Greece into the club. Again, this had nothing to do with economics and everything with symbolism. Greece, the supposed cradle of democracy, may have been an economic basket case for centuries. But Europe without Greece just did not feel right.

There was no shortage of critical voices at the time. Germany's former economics minister Otto Graf Lambsdorff voted against letting Greece into the eurozone when the Bundestag decided on the matter. He warned that Greece was just not ready, but Lambsdorff and hundreds of economics professors writing petitions against the euro were just ignored.

When European Monetary Union started, the rules that were supposed to govern the project were never followed. They were barely worth the paper they were printed on. Deficit and debt rules, the no bailout rule, the mandate to keep the European

Central Bank focussed on just price stability and independent: When push came to shove, none of these rules mattered. The European Union never followed any of them. How on earth were they expecting anyone to develop trust in their actions, let alone the euro?

Various Greek governments deserve a lot of the blame for their country's crisis. It was the mainstream Greek centre-left and centre-right parties that overspent, fiddled their statistics, found ingenious ways of clandestinely borrowing — all the while they proved themselves incapable of reforming their county. Yes, the current Syriza government is a disaster. But to be fair to Tsipras, Varoufakis & co., they inherited a mess of a country.

Other European political leaders are just as guilty of the disaster around Athens. Back in 2010, when it was obvious what a catastrophe the euro had caused in Greece, German Chancellor Angela Merkel briefly wanted to do what is right: kick Greece out of the eurozone. Under pressure from other European countries and the US government, she quickly changed her tune. Ever since, the EU has been trying to fight debt with more debt.

The result of all of this is simple: The private sector managed to get out of Greece while all risks were transferred to European taxpayers. Privatise the gains, socialise the losses. Sorry if I sound like a socialist, but that is precisely what happened.

And what did all of this really achieve? Well, after five years Greece is more, not less indebted than before. Its economy has shrunk by 25 percent since the peak. Its unemployment rate is 26 percent. There is no sign of growth but growing tension between Greece and the rest of Europe.

The only good idea in the bailout process was to engage the International Monetary Fund in the packages. After all, the IMF has the necessary knowledge to turn around countries. However, led by its French directors Dominique Strauss-Kahn and Christine Lagarde, the IMF did not play the role of an independent arbitrator but that of an interested player. Greece became the IMF's largest ever bailout, even though it is a small (and relatively rich) country.

In a world that is becoming more Asian, the IMF became more European. It paid too much attention to Greece and invested way too much money. Had it behaved in a similar way if it had not been about a European country? Had it done the same if it had not been headed by a former French politician? To ask these questions is to answer them.

Finally, the current Greek government. What Tsipras and Varoufakis have delivered in recent months must be the worst ever example of international diplomacy. Announce something one day and propose the opposite a day later. Procrastinate around decision-making and arrive unprepared to important meetings. Threaten European neighbours while asking them for help. Saying one thing in Athens and something completely different in Brussels. Charm Vladimir Putin's Russia and call the IMF a criminal organisation. With no due respect, this Greek government is one of the worst the world has ever seen.

Even the Greek government's seemingly democratic idea of holding a referendum is pure cynicism. Its only purpose is to buy more time. The question on the ballot paper is unintelligible. And no matter what the public's answer will be, it does not change anything about Greece's position in Europe.

Don't get me wrong: I love direct democracy and would like to see more of it. But rather than asking the Greeks if they want to have their cake and eat it, maybe we should ask the Germans whether they want to guarantee more Greek loans?

As I said, this is an unbalanced rant. No-one in this crisis is blameless: not the Greeks, not the Germans, not the European Commission, not the European Central Bank and least of all the International Monetary Fund.

There is only one hope. Now that Greece is finally and officially bankrupt, perhaps we might eventually see something resembling a solution to the crisis. How about Greece exiting the eurozone, devaluing its new currency, default on its debt and reform its economy? I have been arguing this case for five years in this column, and I am not the only economist who has been saying so.

Will European leaders finally listen to us?

Published in Business Spectator (Melbourne), 2 July 2015.
Reproduced with permission.

www.ingramcontent.com/pod-product-compliance
Lightning Source LLC
Chambersburg PA
CBHW050843270326
41930CB00019B/3452